BRISKET COOKBOOK

Top 40 Brisket Recipes

KATYA JOHANSSON

CONTENTS

INTRODUCTION

Brisket is similar to meatloaf, as in it's a straightforward, unglamorous solace sustenance that everybody cases to have the best formula for. The formulas all end up being practically the same, with minor varieties, and they all lead to the same place: a healthy, gut-warming supper that will make them lick your plate toward the end.

Brisket is a cut of meat that originates from the bosom area. It's moderately thin and generally extreme, which implies that long, moderate cooking is the best approach. Numerous individuals support moderate flame broiling for brisket with a firm covering and smoky flavor.

This season of year, notwithstanding, we support braising since it requires almost no exertion and warms our home up with an appetizing, substantial smell. The enchantment of moderate cooking never stops to stun, as the change brisket experiences from a generally modest slice of meat to a feast that actually dissolves in your mouth is genuinely bewildering. In a broiler, this change happens in around 2 1/2 hours for a two-pound cut of brisket. In a moderate cooker on high warmth, about twice that.

Notwithstanding the long cooking time, there are a couple of different procedures that insurance delicate brisket. Search for a cut of brisket that has a pleasant layer of fat on the top; it keeps the meat soggy and delicious while cooking and can simply be trimmed away just before eating on the off chance that it's excessively greasy for your taste.

You'll additionally need to encompass, however not absolutely inundate, the brisket in some kind of fluid as it cooks, which is the thing that separates braising from simmering (no fluid) and stewing (more fluid). Soup, wine or a mix of the two, functions admirably for this. Keep a cover on the brisket while it cooks and oppose looking in on it – in any event for the initial two hours.

1. DELICIOUS BAKED BRISKET

INGREDIENTS

- 8 pounds meat brisket
- 20 cloves garlic
- 2 clusters cilantro
- 1/4 glasses red wine vinegar
- 3 onions, meagerly cut
- 1 tablespoon universally handy flour
- 1 extensive warmth safe nylon oven sack

METHOD

1. Trim the overabundance fat from the brisket. Jab a ton of openings all over brisket with a stick. Briskets are generally long, so cut meat down the middle so it will fit into an extensive, resalable sack with the marinade.
2. In a blender, join garlic, cilantro, and vinegar. Mix until smooth. Empty marinade into resalable sack with the meat. Marinate in the cooler for 24 hours.
3. Preheat oven to 300 degrees F (150 degrees C).
4. Shake flour into biggest size oven cooking sack. Place brisket into pack. Close sack and penetrate as educated on bundle. Layer the onions on top of the brisket, within the sack. Place on preparing dish in the focal point of the oven.
5. Heat in preheated oven until delicate, around 6 hours. Cut meagerly over the grain to serve.

2. AMAZING OKLAHOMA BRISKET

INGREDIENTS

- 1/2 glass honey
- 3 tablespoons soy sauce prepared salt to taste
- 1 (5 pound) hamburger brisket
- 1 cup apple juice prepared salt to taste
- 3/4 glass ketchup
- 1/4 glass stuffed brown sugar
- 2 tablespoons Worcestershire sauce
- 1/4 cup apple juice vinegar prepared salt to taste
- 1/2 teaspoon garlic powder, or to taste

METHOD

1. Preheat the oven to 300 degrees F (150 degrees C). Season the brisket done with prepared salt, and place in a broiling skillet. Pour the squeezed apple over it, and cover firmly with aluminum foil.
2. Cook the brisket for 3 hours in the preheated oven. Try not to look.
3. Set up a flame broil for low warmth. In a little bowl, blend together the honey and soy sauce, and season with prepared salt.
4. At the point when the dish leaves the oven, place it on the preheated flame broil. Barbecue for 30 minutes, turning as often as possible and treating with the honey sauce.
5. Then, in a pan over low warmth, make a grill sauce by joining the ketchup, brown sugar, Worcestershire sauce, juice vinegar, prepared salt, and garlic powder. Cook and

mix over low warmth for 15 minutes without permitting the sauce to bubble. On the off chance that you heat up the sauce, it turns out to be exceptionally vinegary.

6. Give the brisket a chance to rest for around 10 minutes after it falls off the barbecue. Cut and present with the grill sauce.

3. DELICIOUS BEEF BRISKET

INGREDIENTS

- 1 (3 pound) meat brisket, trimmed of fat
- 1 medium onion, daintily cut salt and pepper to taste
- 1 (12 liquid ounce) can beer
- 1 (12 ounce) bottle tomato-based stew sauce
- 3/4 cup pressed cocoa sugar

METHOD

1. Preheat the oven to 325 degrees F (165 degrees C).
2. Season the brisket on all sides with salt and pepper, and place in a glass preparing dish. Spread with a layer of cut onions. In a medium dish, combine the beer, stew sauce, and brown sugar. Pour over the dish. Spread the dish firmly with aluminum foil.
3. Heat for 3 hours in the preheated oven. Expel the aluminum foil, and heat for an extra 30 minutes. Give the brisket a chance to rest and cool somewhat before cutting and coming back to the dish. Warm in the oven with the sauce spooned over the cut meat.

4. AMAZING BLAZING BRISKET

INGREDIENTS

- 5 pounds hamburger brisket
- 2 pounds cut bacon
- 5 cups beer coffee
- 1/4 glass salt 1 glass margarine
- 1/2 cup minced garlic
- 1/2 glass shortening
- 1 pound fatback, cut into little rectangles
- 2 sweet potatoes, quartered
- 1 glass olive oil
- 2 1/2 tablespoons arranged horseradish

METHOD

1. Wrap the brisket totally in bacon cuts, and place into an extensive glass heating dish. Combine the coffee and salt. Pour the coffee blend over the brisket, cover, and marinate in the icebox overnight.
2. In a pan over low warmth, consolidate the spread and minced garlic. Cook blending once in a while until margarine is dissolved, and has turned brilliant. Spread the greater part of the shortening onto within a simmering dish. Place the brisket in the skillet with some the coffee marinade. Lay cuts of the fatback over the dish. Put sweet potatoes around the border of the broiling cup. Pour the garlic margarine over the dish and potatoes. Let stand for 60 minutes. Preheat the oven to 325 degrees F (165 degrees C)

3. Spread the broiling dish with aluminum foil, and prepare for 4 hours in the preheated oven. The inward temperature of the dish ought to be no less than 145 degrees F (62 degrees C) when brought with a meat thermometer. Let stand for 10 minutes before cutting.

4. While you sit tight for the meal, blend together the olive oil and horseradish in a little pot. Cook over low warmth for in any event 30 minutes, then fill a little bowl. This is the plunging sauce for the brisket.

5. TASTY CORNED BEEF AND CABBAGE

INGREDIENTS

- 4 substantial carrots, peeled and cut into pieces
- 10 red potatoes, quartered
- 1 onion, peeled and cut into chomp pieces
- 4 mugs water
- 1 (4 pound) corned meat brisket with flavor
- 6 ounces beer
- 1/2 head cabbage, coarsely cleaved

METHOD

1. Place the carrots, potatoes, and onion into the base of a slow cooker, pour in the water, and place the brisket on top of the vegetables. Pour the beer over the brisket. Sprinkle on the flavors from the bundle, cover, and set the cooker on High.
2. Cook the brisket for around 8 hours. Blend in the cabbage and cook for 1 more hour.

6. WONDERFUL REUBEN DIP

INGREDIENTS

- 1 (16 ounce) cup sauerkraut, depleted
- 1 (8 ounce) bundle cream cheese, diminished
- 2 mugs Swiss cheese
- 2 glasses shredded cooked corned beef
- 1/4 cup Thousand Island dressing

METHOD

1. In a slow cooker, consolidate the sauerkraut, cream cheese, Swiss cheese, corned hamburger and Thousand Island dressing.
2. Cover, and cook on high for 45 minutes in case you're in a rush, low for more in case you're not, or just until hot and cheese is dissolved. Blend at times while cooking. Present with mixed drink rye or wafers.

7. Healthy Corned Beef and Cabbage

Ingredients

- 4 1/2 pounds corned beef brisket
- 5 dark peppercorns
- 1/2 teaspoon garlic powder
- 1 onion, peeled
- 2 inlet leaves 1 squeeze salt
- 1 little head cabbage, cored and cut into wedges
- 6 potatoes, quartered
- 4 carrots, peeled and cut
- 1/4 cup cleaved fresh parsley
- 2 tablespoons margarine

Method

1. In a 6 quart Dutch oven, Place the beef brisket, peppercorns, garlic powder, onion, cove leaves and salt. Fill dish with water to cover everything in addition to one inch. Heat to the point of boiling and cook for 20 minutes. Skim off any deposit that buoys to the top. Diminish warmth to a stew and cook for 2 to 3 hours, until meat can be pulled separated with a fork.
2. Once the meat is done, include the cabbage, potatoes and carrots, squeezing them down into the fluid. Stew for an extra 15 minutes or until the potatoes are delicate. Skim off any oil that rises to the top. Mix in the margarine and parsley. Expel the pot from the warmth.
3. Expel meat from the pot and place onto a serving dish and let rest for 15 minutes. Additionally evacuate

vegetables to a dish and keep warm. Cut meat on the askew contrary to what would be expected. Serve meat on a platter and spoon juices over meat and vegetables

8. Delicious Oklahoma Brisket

Ingredients

- 1/2 cup honey
- 3 tablespoons soy sauce prepared salt to taste
- 1 (5 pound) meat brisket
- 1 glass apple juice prepared salt to taste
- 3/4 cup ketchup
- 1/4 cup pressed brown sugar
- 2 tablespoons Worcestershire sauce
- 1/4 glass apple juice vinegar prepared salt to taste
- 1/2 teaspoon garlic powder, or to taste

Method

1. Preheat the oven to 300 degrees F (150 degrees C). Season the brisket done with prepared salt, and place in a simmering cup. Pour the squeezed apple over it, and cover firmly with aluminum foil.
2. Cook the brisket for 3 hours in the preheated oven. Try not to look.
3. Set up a barbecue for low warmth. In a little bowl, blend together the honey and soy sauce, and season with prepared salt.
4. At the point when the meal leaves the oven, place it on the preheated barbecue. Flame broil for 30 minutes, turning every now and again and treating with the honey sauce.
5. In the interim, in a pot over low warmth, make a grill sauce by consolidating the ketchup, brown sugar,

Worcestershire sauce, juice vinegar, prepared salt, and garlic powder. Cook and mix over low warmth for 15 minutes without permitting the sauce to bubble. In the event that you heat up the sauce, it turns out to be exceptionally vinegary.

6. Give the brisket a chance to rest for around 10 minutes after it falls off the flame broil. Cut and present with the grill sauce.

9. WINE BEEF BRISKET

INGREDIENTS

- 1 teaspoon dried thyme
- 1 teaspoon salt
- 1/4 teaspoon ground dark pepper
- 1 (3 pound) meat brisket
- 1 tablespoon olive oil
- 1 red onion, cut
- 1 (14.5 ounce) can hamburger soup
- 1 (8 ounce) can tomato sauce
- 1/2 glass red wine

METHOD

1. Preheat oven to 350 degrees F (175 degrees C).
2. Blend thyme, salt, and dark pepper in a little bowl and rub the blend over both sides of brisket.
3. Heat olive oil in a broiling cup over medium-high warmth; place brisket in the hot oil and cocoa on both sides, 3 to 4 minutes for each side. Expel brisket from skillet and put aside.
4. Place red onion cuts into the hot simmering dish and cook and mix until onion is marginally mollified, around 2 minutes. Mix in meat soup, tomato sauce, and wine.
5. Place the brisket once more into the broiling dish and cover skillet with foil.
6. Cook the brisket in the preheated oven for 60 minutes; expel foil and treat brisket with dish juices. Place foil back over cooking dish and meal brisket until

exceptionally delicate and cup sauce has thickened, 1/2
to 2 more hours.

10. HAMBURGER BRISKET

INGREDIENTS

- 1 "first cut" hamburger brisket (5 pounds), fat trimmed to 1/4 creep thick
- Coarse salt and naturally ground pepper
- 1/4 glass additional virgin olive oil
- 6 shallots, peeled and divided
- 5 cloves garlic, peeled
- 1/4 glass potato starch
- 1/2 glasses dry white wine, for example, Sauvignon Blanc
- 4 glasses low-sodium chicken soup
- 1/4 glass grainy mustard
- 3 long strips lemon pizzazz, in addition to 2 tablespoons new lemon juice
- 6 sprigs thyme
- 1/2 pounds child Yukon Gold potatoes, thoroughly cleaned
- 4 medium carrots, peeled and cut into 3-inch pieces
- 1 little turnip, peeled and cut into 4 wedges

METHOD

1. Preheat oven to 300 degrees. Liberally season brisket with salt and pepper. Heat 2 tablespoons oil in an expansive Dutch oven over medium-high. Burn brisket until sautéed, 4 to 5 minutes a side; exchange to a plate. Channel fat from pot and dispose of. Decrease warmth to medium; include remaining 2 tablespoons oil, shallots, garlic, and potato starch and cook, mixing, 2 minutes. Blend in wine, scratching up any sautéed bits from base

of pot. Include juices, mustard, get-up-and-go, and thyme; heat to the point of boiling. Include meat and any gathered juices. Cover and exchange to oven; cook 2 hours, 15 minutes.

2. Flip meat over; include vegetables. Cover and keep on cooking until everything is exceptionally delicate, around 45 minutes. (In case you're sparing it for the following day, let cool, then cover and refrigerate overnight. Warm, secured, in a 350 degrees oven until warmed through, around 40 minutes.)

3. Exchange vegetables to a platter and meat to a cutting board; season with salt. Skim fat from fluid in pot. Blend in lemon juice; season with salt and pepper. Cut brisket contrary to what would be expected and serve, with vegetables and sauce

11. Tasty Braised Beef Brisket

Ingredients

- 3 tablespoons canola oil
- 1 (2-pounds) piece meat brisket
- 2 huge white onions, cleaved
- 4 medium carrots, cut into 1-inch pieces
- 4 celery ribs, cut into 1-inch pieces
- 6 garlic cloves
- 1/4 glass juice vinegar
- 1 glass chicken stock or decreased sodium chicken soup
- 1 (28-ounces) can pounded tomatoes

Method

1. Preheat oven to 350°F with rack in lower third.
2. Heat oil in a wide 5-to 6-quart substantial pot over medium-high warmth until it sparkles. Season brisket with 1 tsp each of salt and pepper, then brown brisket, turning once, around 8 minutes absolute. Exchange to a plate.
3. Diminish warmth to medium. Add onions to pot and cook, blending at times, until brilliant cocoa, 12 to 15 minutes. Include carrots, celery, and garlic and cook, mixing once in a while, until brilliant, 10 to 12 minutes.
4. Include vinegar, mixing and scratching up brown bits. Include stock and tomatoes and convey to a stew. Return brisket to pot, settling it in braising (fluid won't cover meat). Spread with a tight-fitting cover and braise in oven until fork-delicate, 3 to 3 1/2 hours.

12. Best Brisket

Ingredients

- 1 10-12-pound entire meat brisket, fat trimmed to 1/4" thickness
- 1/3 cup genuine salt
- 1/3 cup crisply ground dark pepper
- Exceptional hardware:
- A gas flame broil with a full tank of propane and a trickle plate
- 8 mugs all-regular hardwood chips, ideally hickory, for smoking
- A smoker box
- A flame broil or simple thermometer

Method

1. Season the meat an hour prior setting up the flame broil, place brisket on a rimmed preparing sheet. Blend salt and pepper in a little bowl and season the meat on top of (it ought to look like sand adhered to wet skin however without being cakey). Give meat a chance to sit at room temperature for 60 minutes.
2. Prepare your barbecue meanwhile, spray 6 mugs wood chips contributes a dish of water for no less than 30 minutes or overnight. Leave in water all through the cooking procedure. Continue remaining 2 cups chips dry. Light just 1 flame broil burner to medium (if utilizing a 3-burner barbecue, light burner on either end). Ensure dribble plate is vacant, as a ton of fat will render. Place smoker box over the lit burner, include 1/2

cup sprayed wood chips to box, and close flame broil. Change heat as expected to keep temperature at 225-250°F. We prescribe utilizing a stand-alone thermometer, regardless of the possibility that your flame broil has one, to guarantee a precise perusing. Stick it through the hole between the top and base of the barbecue (or set it on the flame broil's upper rack, however this is not perfect, as it requires opening the cover all the more often). The wood chips ought to start to seethe and discharge a constant flow of smoke. To what extent this takes relies on upon how wet your chips are and the warmth of your barbecue. To get more smoke without expanding barbecue heat, add a couple dry chips to the doused ones.

3. Maintain the warmth Place brisket, greasy side up, on flame broil grate as far from lit burner as could reasonably be expected. Spread flame broil and smoke meat, fighting the temptation to open barbecue frequently, as this will bring about the temperature to vary. Conform heat as expected to keep temperature consistent at 225-250°F. Check wood chips at regular intervals or somewhere in the vicinity, and include doused chips by 1/2-cupfuls as expected to keep smoke level consistent.

4. Know when it's set Keep smoking the brisket, turning like clockwork and flipping as required if top or base is shading speedier than the other, until meat is extremely delicate yet not going to pieces and a moment read thermometer embedded into the thickest piece of meat registers 195-205°F, 10-12 hours total.

13. Amazing Beer Brisket

Ingredients

- 1 (3½ pound) brisket, trimmed
- salt and pepper
- 1 onion, cut
- 1 (4-ounce) can tomato glue
- 1 glass grill sauce
- 2 Tablespoons Worcestershire sauce
- 2 Tablespoons Dijon mustard
- 4 cloves minced garlic
- ¼ glass cocoa sugar
- 1½ mugs root lager

Method

1. Trim your brisket on the off chance that it has a great deal of fat. Season well with salt and pepper. Both sides.
2. Add the brisket to an extremely hot skillet. Cocoa on both sides. My slow cooker has sautéing highlight, so I can do it specifically in my slow cooker. The sluggish young lady in me cherishes that I don't need to messy an additional dish.
3. Exchange the brisket to your slow cooker. Spread the top with cut onions.
4. Combine tomato glue, grill sauce, Worcestershire sauce, Dijon, garlic, and brown sugar. Season with salt and pepper.
5. Pour the sauce over the brisket.
6. Pour over root beer.
7. Cover and cook on LOW for 6 hours.

8. Cut and serve.

14. AMAZING BRISKET OF BEEF

INGREDIENTS

- 6-pound first-cut (a.k.a. level cut) meat brisket, trimmed so that a dainty layer of fat remains
- 1 to 2 teaspoons universally handy flour (or matzoh feast)
- Crisply ground dark pepper
- tablespoons corn oil (or other nonpartisan oil)
- 8 medium onions, peeled and thickly cut
- tablespoons tomato glue
- Genuine salt
- 2 to 4 cloves garlic
- 1 carrot, peeled

METHOD

1 Heat the oven to 350°F. Softly tidy the brisket with flour, then sprinkle with pepper to taste. Heat the oil over medium-high warmth in a huge ovenproof enameled cast-iron pot or other substantial pot with a cover sufficiently vast to hold the brisket cozily. Add the brisket to the pot and cocoa on both sides until dried up brown territories show up at first glance here and there, 5 to 7 minutes for each side.

2 Exchange the brisket to a platter, turn up the warmth somewhat, then add the onions to the pot and blend continually with a wooden spoon, scratching up any seared bits adhered to the base of the pot. Cook until the onions have mellowed and built up a rich brown shading however aren't yet caramelized, 10 to 15

minutes. Turn off the warmth and spot the brisket and any amassed juices on top of the onions. Spread the tomato glue over the brisket as though you were icing a cake. Sprinkle with salt and more pepper to taste, then add the garlic and carrot to the pot. Spread the pot, exchange to the oven, and cook the brisket for 1/2 hours.

3 Exchange the brisket to a cutting board and, utilizing a sharp blade, cut the meat over the grain into around 1/8-inch-thick cuts. Return the cuts to the pot, covering them at a point with the goal that you can see a touch of the top edge of every cut. The finished result ought to take after the first unsliced brisket inclining marginally in reverse. Check the seasonings and, if the sauce seems dry, add 2 to 3 teaspoons of water to the pot. Spread the pot and come back to the oven. Bring down the warmth to 325°F and cook the brisket until it is fork-delicate, 1/2 to 2 hours. Check a few times amid cooking to ensure that the fluid is not percolating endlessly. On the off chance that it is, include a couple of more teaspoons of water— however not more. Likewise, every time you check, spoon a portion of the fluid on top of the meal with the goal that it trickles down between the cuts. It is prepared to present with its juices, at the same time, actually, it's surprisingly better the second day. It likewise solidifies

17. Beef Brisket Pot Roast

Ingredients

- 4-5 pound hamburger brisket
- Salt
- 1-2 Tbsp olive oil
- vast onions, cut
- 5-6 garlic cloves, minced
- 1 sprig thyme
- 1 sprig rosemary
- 3-4 straight takes off
- 2 measures of meat stock
- 2-3 substantial carrots, peeled and cut into 1/2 inch pieces
- 1 Tbsp mustard (discretionary)

Method

1. Prepare the brisket for cooking: On one side of the brisket there ought to be a layer of fat, which you need. On the off chance that there are any extensive pieces of fat, cut them off and dispose of them. Expansive bits of fat won't have the capacity to render out totally.
2. Utilizing a sharp blade, score the fat in parallel lines, around 3/4-creep separated. Cut through the fat, not the meat. Rehash the other way to make a cross-hatch design.
3. Salt the brisket well and let it sit at room temperature for 30 minutes.
4. meat brisket-pot-cook technique 600-1 hamburger brisket-pot-broil strategy 600-2

5. Sear the brisket: You'll require a oven verification, thick-bottomed pot with a spread, or Dutch oven, that is sufficiently wide to hold the brisket cook with a little space for the onions.
6. Pat the brisket dry and place it, greasy side down, into the pot and place it on medium high warmth. Cook for 5-8 minutes, delicately sizzling, until the fat side is pleasantly sautéed. (On the off chance that the meal is by all accounts cooking too quick, turn the warmth down to medium. You need a relentless sizzle, not a furious singe.)
7. Turn the brisket over and cook for a couple of minutes more to brown the other side.
8. meat brisket-pot-cook technique 600-3
9. Sauté the onions and garlic: When the brisket has seared, expel it from the pot and put aside. There ought to be a few tablespoons of fat rendered in the pot, if not, include some olive oil.
10. Include the cleaved onions and expansion the warmth to high. Sprinkle somewhat salt on the onions. Sauté, mixing regularly, until the onions are gently caramelized, 5-8 minutes. Blend in the garlic and cook 1-2 more minutes.
11. meat brisket-pot-cook strategy 600-5 hamburger brisket-pot-broil technique 600-4
12. Return brisket to pot, include herbs, stock, and convey to stew, spread, and cook in oven: Preheat the oven to 300°F. Use kitchen twine to entwine the sound leaves, rosemary and thyme.
13. Move the onions and garlic to the sides of the pot and settle the brisket inside. Include the hamburger stock and the tied-up herbs. Heat the stock to the point of boiling on the oven top.
14. Spread the pot, put the pot in the 300°F oven and cook for 3 hours. Deliberately flip the brisket consistently so it cooks uniformly.
15. meat brisket-pot-broil technique 600-6 hamburger brisket-pot-cook strategy 600-7

16. Add carrots, keep on cooking: After 3 hours, include the carrots. Spread the pot and cook for 1 hour more, or until the carrots are cooked through and the brisket is going into disrepair delicate.
17. Remove brisket to cutting board, tent with foil: When the brisket is going to pieces delicate, take the pot out of the oven and evacuate the brisket to a cutting board. Spread it with foil. Haul out and dispose of the herbs.
18. Make sauce (discretionary): At this point you have two alternatives. You can serve as may be, or you can make a sauce with the drippings and a portion of the onions. On the off chance that you serve as may be, avoid this progression.
19. To make a sauce, evacuate the carrots and half of the onions, put aside and spread them with foil. Pour the ingredient s that are staying into the pot into a blender, and purée until smooth. In the event that you need, add 1 tablespoon of mustard to the blend. Put into a little pot and keep warm.
20. Slice the meat over the grain: Notice the lines of the muscle filaments of the dish. This is the grain of the meat. Cut the meat opposite to these lines, or over the grain (cutting along these lines further softens the meat), in 1/4-inch to 1/2-inch cuts.
21. Present with the onions, carrots and sauce. Present with squashed, cooked or bubbled potatoes, egg noodles or polenta.

18. HEALTHY POMEGRANATE BRISKET TACOS

INGREDIENTS

- Pomegranate Shredded Brisket
- 2-3 lb. second cut brisket
- 1 red onion, cut
- ½ glass pomegranate seeds
- ½ glass solidify dried cranberries
- 1 Tbsp garlic powder
- 1 Tbsp paprika
- ½ Tbsp coriander
- 1 tsp salt
- 1 tsp pepper
- ½ tsp cayenne pepper
- ½ tsp cinnamon
- 2 glasses pomegranate juice
- Taco Toppings
- delicate corn tortillas
- pomegranate seeds
- chives
- Cole slaw
- salted red onions

METHOD

1. Preheat the oven to 425 degrees F and line a goulash dish with a layer of foil, making a point to leave a great deal of foil hanging over the sides to wrap the brisket later on.

2. Place the cut onions and pomegranate seeds on the base of the dish and place the dry brisket right on top, fat side up.

3. Squash the stop dried cranberries into a fine powder (you can do this in a sustenance processor) then blend in the majority of the flavors. Pour half of the zest blend on to the brisket and rub it in then flip over the brisket and rub on whatever is left of the zest blend. Flip the brisket more than once again to make certain the fat side is on top. The fat will dissolve into the brisket as it cooks.

4. Wrap the foil firmly around the brisket then place another bit of foil on top of the dish and seal it close.

5. Cook the brisket at 425 degrees F. for 1 hour then lower the temperature to 225 degrees F. what's more, cook for 6-8 more hours. You can do this overnight.

6. When you expel the brisket from the oven, open up the majority of the foil and let the meat cool for 30 minutes. Deliberately pour the juices in the base of the dish through a strainer specifically into an expansive shallow cup. This will evacuate the cooked pomegranate seeds and onion from the fluid. You can include the onions once again into the juice in the event that you need them in your sauce. Pour in the pomegranate juice.

7. Heat the juices over medium warmth until stewing then cook the sauce for around 30 minutes, mixing incidentally, until it has turned out to be thick.

8. While the sauce is thickening, shred the brisket with two forks. At that point you can pour the sauce over the brisket or keep it as an afterthought to shower on the tacos.

9. To gather the tacos, put as abundantly shredded ed brisket on the corn tortillas, top with crisp pomegranate seeds, chives and even cole slaw or cured red onions.

19. HEALTHY PINEAPPLE BRISKET

INGREDIENTS

- Flavor rub
- 1 Tbsp lemon powder
- 2 Tbsp nutmeg
- 2 Tbsp thyme
- 2 Tbsp cinnamon
- 1 Tbsp pepper
- Maple Glaze
- 6 Tbsp maple syrup
- ½ cup cocoa sugar

METHOD

1. Flavor rub
2. Blend ingredient
3. Maple coat
4. Blend ingredient s
5. Brisket
6. Rub brisket with flavor rub
7. Place in slow cooker
8. Place coat over brisket
9. Let cook for no less than 8 hours
10. Barbecue pineapple
11. Serve warm!

20. DELICIOUS SALPICON BEEF SALAD

INGREDIENTS

- lbs hamburger brisket
- 1 onion, quartered
- 1 teas garlic powder
- 1 tbs cumin
- 1 tbs oregano
- 1 teas bean stew powder
- 1 teas salt
- 1 teas pepper
- 2 glasses water
- 3 chipotle peppers in adobo sauce
- 1/2 glass olive oil
- 1 tbs red wine vinegar
- 1 tbs lime juice
- tomatoes, seeded and slashed
- 8 little radishes, cut meager
- 2 avocados, cut meager
- Corn tortillas, warmed
- Shredded ed lettuce
- Queso Fresco
- Salted onions

METHOD

1   Place brisket in a Dutch oven with onion, garlic powder, cumin, oregano, stew powder, salt and pepper. Add enough water to cover brisket. Cover and heat to the

point of boiling over high warmth. Diminish to a stew and let do its thing for around 4 hours, until meat effortlessly pulls separated.

2　Deliberately expel hamburger from Dutch oven and spot in a dish. Shred with two forks, cover and put aside. Dispose of fluid and onion.

3　Puree the chipotle peppers in a nourishment processor. Hurl the olive oil, vinegar, chipotle peppers, lime juice, tomatoes, and radishes together. Add meat and hurl to join. Season with salt and pepper as required. Cover and refrigerate no less than 2 hours before serving. Hurl again before serving and check for flavoring.

4　Serve over shredded ed lettuce with warmed tortillas and extra garnishes as fancied, for example, queso fresco, salted onions, diced tomatoes.

21. TRAEGER AMAZING BRISKET

INGREDIENTS

- 1 (6-8 LB.) BRISKET
- traeger's beef shake
- prime rib rub
- salt and pepper

METHOD

1 For a 6 to 8 lb. brisket, plan for 8 to 12 hours of cook time, approximately a hour and a half for every lb. A remote test thermometer is basic to use for brisket.
2 Coat brisket generously with favored rub, Traeger Beef Rub, Prime Rib Rub, or salt and pepper then, wrap in plastic wrap.
3 Give the wrapped brisket a chance to sit 12 to 24 hours in the fridge.
4 Permit a lot of time for cooking. At the point when prepared to cook, begin the Traeger flame broil on Smoke with the cover open until the flame is built up (4 to 5 minutes). Leave temperature set to Smoke, and pre-heat, cover shut (10-15 minutes).
5 Place brisket fat side up on the flame broil grate, embed thermometer test and smoke for 4 hours.
6 Following 4 hours turn barbecue up to 250F.
7 At the point when inward meat temperature achieves 180F, expel brisket from the flame broil and wrap in foil - DO NOT evacuate thermometer test.
8 Place foiled brisket back on barbecue and cook until interior temperature is 200-205F.

9   Evacuate brisket and permit it to rest in the foil for no less than 30 minutes.

22. Amazing Brisket

Ingredients

- 2 teaspoons ground cumin
- 2 teaspoons sweet Hungarian paprika
- 1/2 teaspoon dried thyme
- 1/4 teaspoons genuine salt, partitioned
- 2 1/2 pounds level cut hamburger brisket, trimmed
- 1 tablespoon olive oil
- 1/2 mugs pale beer
- mugs lower-sodium meat soup
- garlic cloves, cut
- carrots, cut askew into 1/2-inch pieces
- 6 celery stalks, cut askew into 1/2-inch pieces
- 2 medium onions, every cut into 12 wedges
- 2 tablespoons universally handy flour
- 1/2 glass water

Method

1 Preheat oven to 325°.
2 Consolidate initial 3 ingredient s in a little bowl; mix in 1 teaspoon salt. Rub flavor blend uniformly over both sides of brisket. Heat a Dutch oven over medium-high warmth. Add oil to dish; whirl to coat. Include brisket; sauté 3 minutes every side or until cooked. Expel brisket from dish. Include beer; heat to the point of boiling, scratching cup to relax seared bits. Include stock and garlic; come back to a bubble. Return brisket to dish. Cover and cook at 325° for 2 hours. Turn brisket over; cook an extra 2 hours. Turn brisket over. Add carrot,

celery, and onion; cook an extra 1 hour or until brisket is exceptionally delicate.

3 Expel brisket and vegetables from cup utilizing an opened spoon. Skim fat from cooking fluid; dispose of fat. Heat cooking fluid to the point of boiling over medium-high warmth. Place flour in a little bowl; mix in 1/2 cup water. Add flour blend to skillet, mixing until smooth; heat to the point of boiling, mixing continually. Cook 2 minutes or until somewhat thickened. Mix in remaining 1/4 teaspoon salt. Serve the sauce with meat and vegetables.

23. DELICIOUS BARBACOA BRISKET

INGREDIENTS

- 1 tablespoon finely sliced new oregano
- 1 tablespoon dull brown sugar
- 2 tablespoons olive oil
- 1 tablespoon minced chipotle chilies in adobo sauce
- 1 tablespoon adobo sauce
- 1 teaspoon ground cumin
- 3/4 teaspoon legitimate salt
- 1/2 teaspoon newly ground dark pepper
- garlic cloves, ground
- 1 pound trimmed meat brisket
- 2 medium tomatoes, sliced (around 2 mugs)
- 1/2 medium onion, sliced (around 1 cup)
- 1 red chime pepper, cleaved (around 1 glass)
- 1 jalapeño pepper, seeded and sliced

METHOD

1 Mix initial 9 ingredient s (through garlic) in a medium dish, mixing great to join. Rub blend into brisket.
2 Organize tomatoes, onion, chime pepper, and jalapeño in the base of a 6-quart slow cooker. Place the brisket on top of vegetables, and sprinkle any remaining flavor blend over brisket and vegetables. Cover and cook on LOW for 8 hours.

3　Expel the brisket from the slow cooker, and shred meat with 2 forks. Return brisket to cooker, and hurl with the vegetables.

24. Tasty Sweet and Tangy Brisket

Ingredients

- 1 (4 1/2-pound) flat cut brisket roast, fat top trimmed to 1/8-inch thickness
- 1/4 teaspoons kosher salt, separated
- 1/2 teaspoon crisply ground dark pepper
- 1 tablespoon canola oil
- 1/2 teaspoons garlic powder
- 1 teaspoon paprika
- medium carrots, peeled and cut into thirds
- celery stalks, cut into thirds
- Cooking spray
- 2 extensive onions, split and vertically cut
- garlic cloves, cleaved
- 1 cup unsalted meat stock, (for example, Swanson)
- 1 (15-ounce) can pulverized tomatoes
- 2 tablespoons brown sugar
- 2 tablespoons juice vinegar
- thyme sprigs
- 2 narrows clears out
- Level leaf parsley leaves

Method

1 Sprinkle brisket equitably with 1 teaspoon salt and pepper. Heat a substantial skillet over medium-high warmth. Include oil; whirl to coat. Include brisket; cook 5 minutes, swinging to brown on all sides. Rub brisket

with garlic powder and paprika. Orchestrate carrots and celery in a 6-quart electric slow cooker covered with cooking spray; top with brisket, fat top side up.

2   Return skillet to medium warmth. Add onions to skillet; cover and cook 10 minutes, mixing sometimes. Reveal. Blend in garlic; cook 5 minutes or until onions are delicate and brilliant. Organize onion blend over brisket.

3   Join remaining 1/4 teaspoon salt, stock, tomatoes, brown sugar, and vinegar in hot skillet, mixing with a race to extricate sautéed bits. Pour tomato blend around brisket. Place thyme and cove leaves in slow cooker, squeezing into tomato blend. Cover and cook on LOW for 7 hours or until brisket is delicate when cut. Cool marginally in cooker, around 60 minutes.

4   Place brisket on a cutting board. Trim fat top; dispose of fat. Cut brisket over the grain into flimsy cuts. Pour sauce through a sifter over a dish; dispose of carrots, celery, thyme, and sound takes off. Return onions to sauce. Serve brisket with sauce. Trim with crisp parsley, if coveted.

25. BARBECUE BRISKET SANDWICHES

INGREDIENTS

- 1 glass cut onion, isolated into rings
- 3/4 glass packaged bean stew sauce
- 1/2 glass lager
- 1 tablespoon Worcestershire sauce
- 1 (2 1/2-pound) hamburger brisket
- 1 teaspoon dark pepper
- garlic cloves, minced
- 1/4 glass pressed brown sugar
- 8 (2 1/2-ounce) submarine rolls

METHOD

1   Join initial 4 ingredient s in a 6-quart weight cooker. Heat to the point of boiling; lessen warmth, and stew 5 minutes. Expel 1/2 measure of stew sauce blend from weight cooker.
2   Trim fat from brisket. Sliced brisket down the middle across. Rub the brisket with pepper and garlic. Place in weight cooker. Spoon 1/2 cup bean stew sauce blend over brisket. Close top safely; convey to high weight over high warmth (around 5 minutes). Conform the warmth to medium or level expected to keep up high weight; cook 60 minutes.
3   Expel from warmth; place weight cooker under chilly running water. Evacuate cover. Expel brisket from weight cooker, and put aside. Add the cocoa sugar to bean stew sauce blend in weight cooker; heat to the point

of boiling. Diminish warmth, and stew, revealed, for 5 minutes, mixing every now and again. Shred the brisket utilizing 2 forks. Return meat to sauce in weight cooker; cook until completely warmed. Spoon 1 cup meat with sauce over base of every roll, and cover with highest points of rolls.

26. Coffee Texas-Style Brisket

Ingredients

- mugs oak or hickory wood chips
- 1 tablespoon ground coffee
- 1 tablespoon legitimate salt
- 1 tablespoon dull cocoa sugar
- 2 teaspoons smoked paprika
- 2 teaspoons ancho chili powder
- 1 teaspoon garlic powder
- 1 teaspoon onion powder
- 1 teaspoon ground cumin
- 1 teaspoon newly ground dark pepper
- 1 (4 1/2-pound) level cut brisket (around 3 creeps thick)

Method

1. Spray the wood chips contributes water no less than 60 minutes; channel.
2. Consolidate coffee and the following 8 ingredient s in a dish. Pat brisket dry; rub with coffee blend.
3. Expel barbecue rack, and put aside. Plan barbecue for aberrant flame broiling, warming one side to high and abandoning one side with no warmth. Penetrate base of an expendable aluminum foil dish a few times with the tip of a blade. Place cup on warmth component on warmed side of barbecue; include 1/2 mugs wood chips to dish. Place another expendable aluminum foil cup (don't penetrate dish) on unheated side of flame broil.

Pour 2 mugs water in skillet. Give chips a chance to remain for 15 minutes or until smoking; diminish warmth to medium-low. Keep up temperature at 225°. Place barbecue rack on flame broil. Place the brisket in a little cooking cup, and spot skillet on flame broil rack on unheated side. Close cover; cook for 6 hours or until a meat thermometer registers 195°. Include 1/2 cups wood chips each hour for initial 4 hours; spread dish with foil for remaining 2 hours. Expel from barbecue. Let stand, secured, 30 minutes.

4 Unwrap brisket, holding juices; trim and dispose of fat. Place an extensive zip-top plastic sack inside a 4-cup glass measure. Empty juices through a sifter into sack; dispose of solids. Give drippings a chance to remain for 10 minutes (fat will ascend to the top). Seal pack; painstakingly cut off 1 base corner of sack. Channel drippings into a dish, ceasing before fat achieves opening; dispose of fat. Cut brisket crosswise over grain into slight cuts; present with juices.

27. Tasty Beef Brisket with Beer

Ingredients

- 1 (3-pound) meat brisket, trimmed
- 1 teaspoon salt
- 1/2 teaspoon newly ground dark pepper
- Cooking spray
- 1/4 cup water
- 2 cups vertically cut onion (around 1 expansive)
- 1/2 cups slashed parsnip (around 2)
- 1 tablespoon balsamic vinegar
- 1 straight leaf
- 1 (12-ounce) bottle light beer

Method

1 Rub brisket with salt and pepper. Heat a substantial overwhelming skillet over medium-high warmth. Coat dish with cooking spray. Add brisket to dish; cook 10 minutes, searing on all sides. Expel brisket from the dish. Include 1/4 cup water to skillet, mixing to slacken sautéed bits. Include onion and parsnip; sauté 5 minutes or until vegetables are delicate.
2 Place onion blend, vinegar, straight leaf, and lager in an extensive electric slow cooker. Place brisket on top of onion blend. Cover and cook on low for 8 hours. Dispose of inlet leaf. Cut brisket corner to corner over the grain into dainty cuts. Present with sauce.

28. Braised Brisket & Honey Glaze

Ingredients

- teaspoons canola oil
- 1 (5-pound) level cut meat brisket, trimmed
- 1 teaspoon legitimate salt, separated
- 1 teaspoon newly ground dark pepper
- cups water
- cups dull lager
- 2 cups sliced carrot
- 1 cup vertically cut onion
- 1/4 cup sliced peeled crisp ginger
- 1/4 cup no-salt-included ketchup
- 1 teaspoon lower-sodium soy sauce
- 1/4 teaspoon pounded red pepper
- 20 cilantro sprigs
- thyme sprigs
- orange skin strips
- lemon skin strips
- 2 straight clears out
- 1 apple, cored and cut into 6 wedges
- 1 (3-inch) cinnamon stick
- 1/4 glass honey
- tablespoons crisp lime juice
- 1/4 glass slashed crisp cilantro

Method

1   Preheat oven to 325°.

2   Heat oil in a substantial simmering skillet over medium-high warmth. Sprinkle hamburger with 3/4 teaspoon salt and dark pepper. Add meat to dish; cook 15 minutes, searing on both sides. Channel oil from dish. Include water and next 14 ingredient s (through cinnamon). Heat to the point of boiling; cover with foil, and prepare at 325° for 4 hours. Expel hamburger from skillet, holding cooking fluid. Strain fluid through a sifter into a dish, and skim fat from surface. Return fluid and hamburger to skillet.

3   Cook hamburger, revealed, at 325° for 1/2 to 2 hours or until meat is fork-delicate, treating incidentally. Expel meat from dish, saving cooking fluid; cover and keep warm.

4   Place an expansive zip-top plastic sack inside a dish. Empty cooking fluid into sack. Painstakingly cut off 1 base corner of sack, and deplete fluid into a medium pot, halting before fat layer achieves opening. Dispose of fat. Cook the fluid over medium-high warmth until diminished to around 1 glass. Blend in remaining 1/4 teaspoon salt, honey, and lime juice. Cut meat slantingly crosswise over grain into slim cuts; present with sauce. Sprinkle equally with slashed cilantro.

29. BRISKET WITH OLIVES & LEMONS

INGREDIENTS

- 1 (2 1/2-pound) hamburger brisket, trimmed
- garlic cloves
- 1 teaspoon fit salt
- 1/2 teaspoon naturally ground dark pepper
- Cooking shower
- 8 glasses slashed onion (around 4 expansive)
- 1/2 cup water
- 1/3 cup diced celery
- teaspoons ground peeled new ginger
- 1/2 teaspoon ground turmeric
- 1/8 teaspoon white pepper
- 1 (14.5-ounce) can stewed tomatoes, undrained
- 2 sound takes off
- 1/4 cup coarsely cleaved new parsley, partitioned
- 1/4 cup coarsely cleaved new cilantro, partitioned
- 1/4 cup finely cleaved Preserved Lemons
- 1/3 cup oil-cured olives, set and daintily cut

METHOD

1 Preheat oven to 350°.
2 Make 5 (1/2-inch-profound) openings into brisket; place 1 garlic clove in every opening. Sprinkle brisket equally with salt and dark pepper.
3 Heat a huge nonstick skillet over medium-high warmth. Coat skillet with cooking shower. Add brisket to cup;

cook 5 minutes, caramelizing on all sides. Expel from cup.

4   Recoat dish with cooking shower. Add onion to cup; sauté 10 minutes or until delicate. Include 1/2 glass water and next 6 ingredient s (through cove leaves) to cup; cook 2 minutes or until warmed through.

5   Place brisket in a 13 x 9–inch preparing dish covered with cooking shower; top with onion blend. Spread dish with foil. Heat at 350° for 3 hours or until brisket is extremely delicate. Expel brisket from dish, saving onion blend. Dispose of straight takes off. Blend 2 tablespoons parsley and 2 tablespoons cilantro into onion blend.

6   Cut brisket corner to corner crosswise over grain into slight cuts. Mastermind brisket and onion blend on a serving platter; sprinkle with remaining 2 tablespoons parsley and remaining 2 tablespoons cilantro. Present with Preserved Lemons and olives.

30. Tasty Braised Brisket with Onion

Ingredients

- 1/2 teaspoons salt, partitioned
- 1 teaspoon ground cumin
- 3/4 teaspoon crisply ground dark pepper
- 1/2 teaspoon smoked paprika
- garlic cloves, minced
- tablespoons canola oil, separated
- 1 (4 1/2-pound) flat cut brisket roast (untrimmed)
- cups unsalted hamburger stock
- 1 (12-ounce) beer
- medium onions, cut
- tablespoons juice vinegar
- 2 tablespoons brown sugar
- 1/2 teaspoons cornstarch
- 1/2 tablespoons sliced crisp thyme

Method

1. Preheat oven to 325°.
2. Consolidate 1/4 teaspoons salt and next 4 ingredient s (through garlic) in a little bowl. Blend in 1 tablespoon oil. Rub salt blend equally over side of meat without fat top; place hamburger, salt-blend side down, in an enameled cast-iron Dutch oven. Consolidate stock and beer; pour over meat. Cover and heat at 325° for 4 hours or until delicate, turning following 2 hours. Cool to room temperature; cover and refrigerate overnight.

3 Preheat oven to 350°.

4 Trim fat top from meat; dispose of. Daintily cut hamburger. Skim fat from cooking fluid; dispose of fat. Expel 1 cup cooking fluid; put aside. Place hamburger and remaining cooking fluid in a 13 x 9-inch glass or clay preparing dish; spread with foil. Prepare at 350° for 30 minutes or until completely warmed.

5 Heat a huge skillet over medium-high warmth. Add remaining 2 tablespoons oil to dish; whirl to coat. Include onions; sauté 6 minutes. Decrease warmth to medium; cook 15 minutes or until delicate, mixing once in a while. Blend in vinegar, sugar, and cornstarch; cook 30 seconds. Mix in saved 1 glass cooking fluid; heat to the point of boiling. Cook 1 minute, blending every now and again; expel from warmth. Mix in remaining 1/4 teaspoon salt and thyme. Present with hamburger.

31. Braised Beef Brisket with Onions and Potatoes

Ingredients

- glasses zinfandel or other fruity dry red wine
- 1/2 glass sans fat, less-sodium chicken soup
- 1/4 glass tomato glue
- 1 (2 1/2-pound) hamburger brisket, trimmed
- 2 teaspoons salt, isolated
- 1/2 teaspoon naturally ground dark pepper, isolated
- Cooking shower
- glasses cut Walla or other sweet onion (around 4 medium)
- 2 tablespoons sugar
- 1/4 teaspoons dried thyme, isolated
- garlic cloves, meagerly cut
- 2 carrots, peeled and cut into (1/2-inch-thick) cuts
- 2 celery stalks, cut into (1/2-inch-thick) cuts
- 1/2 pounds little red potatoes, cut into quarters
- 1/2 teaspoons extra virgin olive oil
- 1 teaspoon dried oregano
- 1/4 teaspoon ground red pepper
- Sliced new parsley

Method

1 Preheat oven to 325°.
2 Consolidate initial 3 ingredient s, mixing with a whisk.
3 Heat an extensive Dutch oven over medium-high warmth. Sprinkle meat with 3/4 teaspoon salt and 1/4

teaspoon dark pepper. Coat cup with cooking spray. Add hamburger to cup; cook for 8 minutes, searing on all sides. Expel hamburger from skillet; cover and put aside.

4 Include 1/2 teaspoon salt, 1/4 teaspoon dark pepper, onion, sugar, and 1 teaspoon thyme to dish. Cook 20 minutes or until onions are delicate and brilliant brown, mixing once in a while. Include garlic, carrots, and celery; cook 5 minutes, mixing once in a while. Place meat on top of onion blend; pour wine blend over hamburger. Cover and place in oven.

5 Heat at 325° for 1 3/4 hours.

6 While hamburger blend cooks, place potatoes in a huge dish. Include 3/4 teaspoon salt, 1/4 teaspoon thyme, oil, oregano, and red pepper; hurl to coat. Organize in a solitary layer on a jam move dish covered with cooking spray.

7 Expel hamburger from oven; turn meat over. Place potatoes on lower rack in oven. Spread meat; come back to oven. Prepare potatoes and hamburger at 325° for 45 minutes or until meat is delicate. Expel meat from oven; cover and keep warm. Build oven temperature to 425°. Place potatoes on center rack in oven; heat at 425° for 15 minutes or until fresh and edges are cooked.

8 Expel hamburger from cup; cut over the grain into slight cuts. Present with onion blend and potatoes. Sprinkle with parsley.

32. Tasty Barbecued Brisket Sandwiches

Ingredients

- onions, meagerly cut and partitioned
- 1 (3-pound) hamburger brisket
- 1 teaspoon ground pepper
- 1/4 teaspoon salt
- 2 tablespoons universally handy flour
- 1 (12-ounce) bottle bean stew sauce
- 1/2 glass light lager
- 2 tablespoons cocoa sugar
- 1 tablespoon arranged horseradish
- 1 tablespoon minced garlic (around 6 cloves)
- submarine moves, split and toasted

Method

1   Put half of onion rings in base of a 4-quart electric slow cooker. Trim fat from meat, and slice into expansive pieces to fit in slow cooker; sprinkle with pepper and salt. Dig meat in flour; place on top of onion, sprinkling with any remaining flour. Include staying half of onion.

2   Consolidate bean stew sauce and next 4 ingredients in a medium dish, blending admirably. Pour over meat blend. Cover and cook on high 4 to 5 hours or until meat is delicate. Evacuate brisket, and supplant slow cooker spread.

3   Shred hamburger, utilizing 2 forks; return meat to hot
    fluid in slow cooker, mixing great. Spoon meat blend
    over toasted move parts.

33. Smoked Tasty Brisket

Ingredients

- 5 pounds hamburger brisket, trimmed of fat
- 3 tablespoons mustard, or as required
- 2 tablespoons brisket rub

Method

1. First coat meat brisket with mustard. Spread with brisket rub. Let marinate in the refrigerator, 8 hours to overnight.
2. Take out brisket from the fridge and keep in room temperature.
3. Preheat a smoker to 220 degrees F (104 degrees F).
4. Put hamburger brisket in the smoker and smoke till penetrated with a blade and a moment read thermometer embedded into the middle peruses 190 degrees F (88 degrees C), 6 1/4 to 7 1/2 hours.
5. Wrap brisket with aluminum foil and let rest for 30 minutes before cutting.

34. SPICY DELICIOUS BEEF BRISKET

INGREDIENTS

- Joint of brisket (unrolled)
- Spicy Rub - one of our off the rack rubs by Quiet Waters or Gordon Rhodes, or make your own
- Can of cola
- Baste: 200g muscovado sugar, 100ml juice vinegar
- A powerful chunk smoke flavor - attempt oak, whisky oak or mesquite chunk chips

METHOD

1. Select a brisket with a 5mm layer of white fat and marbling going through the meat. This renders out cooking and helps the meat stay wet and delicate.
2. Marinade the meat utilizing a marinade injector with cola. An unusual ingredient you may think, however one which successfully separates a portion of the meat tendons for a more delicate result. Make numerous little entry points instead of infusing in extensive sums without a moment's delay.
3. Brush the meat with oil and afterward coat generously with a hot rub. Wrap in Clingfilm and leave overnight in the cooler.
4. Convey to room temperature whilst setting up your smoker or grill. Build up the coals and if utilizing a grill, position these to the other side for roundabout cooking.
5. Place the meat on the flame broil rack and cook at 110°C at a rate of 1 and a quarter hours for each lb. of meat.

6. You can likewise make a season, which ought to be connected hourly, however you can effectively cook brisket without one. Blend muscovado sugar with juice vinegar and include a tad bit of any remaining zest rub.
7. At the point when the inner temperature comes to around 90°C the meat is cooked. Wrap the meat in foil and leave for a further hour or thereabouts.
8. Expel from the smoker and permit to rest.
9. Cut daintily, contrary to what would be expected and serve.

35. Delicious Spicy Brisket

Ingredients

- 1 packer brisket split between flat and point
- 1 bottle Patriot's BBQ beef and shoulder rub
- 3 to 6 ounces spicy brown mustard
- Apple juice for basting and wash
- Beer for cooking and wash

Method

1. Separate fat from the separated pieces top 1/4 inch or less. Slather meat with spicy brown mustard. Rub meat with the dry rub. Wrap and let rest for 8 to 12 hours. Set your Masterbuilt smoker to 230 F. Foil the water tray to make clean up easier. Add a mixture of hot water, beer and apple juice to the wash. Smoke it.
2. Add small amounts of chunk at a time until the meat hits an internal temperature of 140 degrees. After smoke, start spritzing the meat with apple juice every two hours, until the meat hits 165 degrees.
3. Foil the meat with one last spritz of apple juice. Continue to cook till the internal temperature gets to 195 degrees. Remove from your Masterbuilt smoker, wrap in towels and rest in an insulated container for a minimum of 30 minutes. Two hours is best. Slice and enjoy!

36. AMAZING BRISKET WITH APPLE JUICE

INGREDIENTS

- 1 packer brisket split between flat and point
- 1 bottle Patriot's BBQ beef and shoulder rub
- 3 to 6 ounces spicy brown mustard
- Apple juice for basting
- Beer for cooking

METHOD

4. Trim brisket to separate the flat from the point. Trim fat from the separated pieces top 1/4 inch or less. Slather meat with spicy brown mustard. Rub meat generously with the dry rub. Wrap and let rest for 8 to 12 hours. Set you Masterbuilt smoker to 230 degrees. Foil the water tray to make clean up easier. Add a mixture of hot water, beer and apple juice to the wash. Smoke with your favorite woods.

5. Keep adding small amounts of wood at a time until the meat hits an internal temperature of 140 degrees. After hour 2 of the smoke, start spritzing the meat with apple juice every two hours, until the meat hits 165 degrees.

6. Foil the meat with one last spritz of apple juice. Continue to cook until the internal temperature gets to 195 degrees. Remove from your Masterbuilt smoker, wrap in towels and rest in an insulated container for a minimum of 30 minutes. Two hours is best. Slice and enjoy! Note: Average brisket time is 13 to 15 hours with a few going longer. This is only an estimate because every brisket is

different. Cooking by temperature is the only way to cook brisket properly.

37. Delicious Smoked Brisket

Ingredients

- 1.5 lb. meat brisket
- 2 tbsp. maple sugar, date sugar, or coconut sugar
- 2 tsp. smoked ocean salt
- 1 tsp. dark pepper
- 1 tsp. mustard powder
- 1 tsp. onion powder
- ½ tsp. smoked paprika
- 2 c. bone soup or supply of decision
- 1 tbsp. fluid smoke
- 3 new thyme sprigs

Method

1. Expel the brisket from the icebox around 30 minutes before cooking. Pat it dry with paper towels and put it aside.
2. Blend the flavor mix by consolidating the maple sugar, smoked ocean salt, pepper, mustard powder, onion powder, and smoked paprika. Coat the meat liberally on all sides. The rub will get somewhat sticky because of the sugar.
3. Set your Ingredients Pot to "Sauté" and permit it to warm up for 2-3 minutes. Oil the base with a touch of high warmth cooking oil and include the brisket. Chestnut on all sides until profoundly brilliant yet not smoldered. Turn the brisket to greasy side up and include the stock, fluid smoke, and thyme to the

Ingredients Pot. Scratch the sautéed bits off the base and cover with the top.

4. Switch the setting to "Manual" and expansion the cook time to 50 minutes. Once completed, permit the Ingredients Pot to discharge steam all alone (EDIT: I've found that utilizing the snappy discharge valve can leave substantial, leaner cuts of meat tasting somewhat dry). Expel the brisket from the pot and cover it with foil to rest. Switch the Ingredients Pot to "Saute" again to diminish and thicken the sauce (discretionary) with the top off for around 10 minutes.

5. Cut the brisket on a predisposition and serve it with your most loved whipped veg (this formula for Creamy Whipped Parsnips appeared here) and sprinkle with the diminished sauce.

38. AMAZING BONELESS BRISKET

INGREDIENTS

- 2½ pounds boneless meat short ribs, hamburger brisket, or hamburger toss cook slice into 1½-to 2-inch solid shapes
- 1 tablespoon bean stew powder
- 1½ teaspoons fit salt (Diamond Crystal brand)
- 1 tablespoon ghee or fat of decision
- 1 medium onion, meagerly cut
- 1 tablespoon tomato glue
- 6 garlic cloves, peeled and crushed
- ½ glass simmered tomato salsa
- ½ glass bone juices
- ½ teaspoon Red Boat Fish Sauce
- Naturally ground dark pepper
- ½ glass minced cilantro (discretionary)
- 2 radishes, meagerly cut (discretionary)

METHOD

1. In a big dish, consolidate cubed hamburger, stew powder, and salt.
2. Press the "Sauté" catch on your Ingredients Pot and add the ghee to the cooking embed. Once the fats liquefied, include the onions and sauté until translucent.
3. Blend in the tomato glue and garlic, and cook for 30 seconds or until fragrant.
4. Hurl in the prepared hamburger and pour in the salsa, stock, and fish sauce.

5. Cover and bolt the top and press the "Keep Warm/Cancel" catch on the Ingredients Pot. Press the "Meat/Stew" catch to change to the instant cooking mode. In the event that your solid shapes are littler than mine, you can press the "less" catch to diminish the cooking time from the preset 35 minutes. Once the pot is modified, leave.
6. At the point when the stew is done cooking, the Ingredients Pot will change naturally to a "Keep Warm" mode. In case you're utilizing a stove-top instant cooker rather, expel the pot from the warmth. In either case, let the instant discharge actually (~15 minutes).
7. Open the top and season to taste with salt and pepper.

39. WONDERFUL CORNED BEEF AND CABBAGE

INGREDIENTS

- corned hamburger brisket (2-3 lbs)
- 3 mugs hamburger stock
- 4 straight clears out
- 4 entire cloves
- 1 tsp entire white peppercorns (dark peppercorns alright)
- 1/2 tsp mustard seeds
- 2 drops fluid smoke
- 1 head green cabbage, cut into expansive lumps
- 4 carrots, cut into nibble measured lumps
- 4 chestnut or Yukon gold potatoes, peeled and cut into nibble measured lumps

METHOD

1. Add the brisket to the Ingredients Pot; include the juices, narrows leaves, cloves, peppercorns, mustard seeds, and fluid smoke, then add enough water to simply almost cover the brisket. Cover and set to "Meat/Stew" under high instant for 55 minutes. Once completed, permit it to depressurize actually, around 15 minutes, then evacuate the spread. As it depressurizes, cut up the cabbage, carrots, and potatoes in case you're utilizing them.
2. Exchange the fluid from the Ingredients Pot into a stockpot, pouring the fluid through a strainer to get the peppercorns, cloves, and inlet clears out. Keep the meat in the Ingredients Pot, spread it, and turn it off; it'll stay

warm as we set up the vegetables. Add the carrots and potatoes to the fluid in the stockpot and heat to the point of boiling over med/high warmth; once bubbling, include the cabbage, diminish warmth to low, and cover. Stew until the vegetables are delicate, around 20 minutes, then taste and include salt if necessary.

3. Cut the brisket and present with the vegetables and soup.

40. AMAZING CAMP BEEF

INGREDIENTS

- 1/4 c of paprika
- Tbsp of garlic, minced
- Tbsp of thyme
- Tbsp of basil
- Tbsp of oregano
- Tbsp of dried parsley
- Tbsp of ground black pepper
- 1/2 tsp of cayenne
- 1/2 tsp of ground nutmeg
- Tbsp of Tabasco sauce
- Tbsp of Worcestershire sauce
- 3-4 lb. of beef brisket

METHOD

1 Combine all the spices and rub the meat. Now coat with Tabasco and Worcestershire sauce. Refrigerate it for 3 - 5 days.
2 Put meat trivet in bottom of Dutch. Put brisket on trivet. Raise the meat to the highest hook when sizzle and cook over low fire for approx. 12 hours

57819339R30042

Made in the USA
Middletown, DE
03 August 2019